J. ALDEN WEIR, AN AMERICAN PRINTMAKER, 1852-1919

Janet A. Flint, Curator
Department of Prints and Drawings
National Collection of Fine Arts

Published for Brigham Young University and the National Collection of Fine Arts, Smithsonian Institution, Washington, D.C.
By Brigham Young University Press, Provo, Utah, 1972

May 5-June 4, 1972
NATIONAL COLLECTION OF FINE ARTS
Smithsonian Institution
Washington, D.C.

June 20-July 10, 1972
COLUMBUS MUSEUM OF FINE ARTS
Columbus, Ohio

September 1-October 1, 1972
BRIGHAM YOUNG UNIVERSITY
Provo, Utah

Library of Congress Catalog Card Number 72-1781
To be cited as follows:
National Collection of Fine Arts, Smithsonian Institution, Janet A. Flint.
J. Alden Weir, An American Printmaker.
Provo, Utah: Brigham Young University Press, 1972.

Designed by Elizabeth Sur
Photography by Eleanor A. Snyder, NCFA Office of Photography
COVER *Neighboring Farm,* catalog number 42
FRONTISPIECE *Woman in Black,* catalog number 7

Contents

Foreword

J. Alden Weir belonged to that fortunate group of American artists for whom art was an accepted and respected way of life, a life set apart from the humdrum norms of society not by bohemian excess but by greater refinement of judgment and sensibility. Caught up like his friends in new perceptions of nature and strongly opposed to routine academic standards, he nonetheless saw himself as an artist in the timeless tradition; in art the past was no less actual than the present. He collected and savored earlier art with the same freshness of eye that he explored the niceties of his domestic environment. Weir's prints in particular bear out his sense for the craft of art that triumphs over the casual impression or unbridled gesture. He did not exploit technique as such or cultivate a breathless facility. It is, rather, as if the process itself, the resistance of the material—and his drypoints are among his finest works—gave artistic stability to the seemingly casual sketch, providing that poise so basic to his life and work.

We are much indebted to Brigham Young University for prompting this reexamination of Weir's graphic works and for assistance in organizing the exhibition.

JOSHUA C. TAYLOR, Director
National Collection of Fine Arts

Acknowledgments

The College of Fine Arts and Communication at Brigham Young University, in cooperation with the National Collection of Fine Arts, Smithsonian Institution, is pleased to present this exhibition of prints by J. Alden Weir.

The Weir Collection came to the University following the death in 1957 of Mahonri Young who was an artist of broad interest and a close associate and son-in-law of J. Alden Weir, as well as the grandson of Brigham Young. The University's Weir Collection consists of manuscripts, paintings, drawings and prints, in what is perhaps the largest single group of this important American artist's work.

We are grateful to Dr. Joshua C. Taylor, Director of the National Collection; Donald R. McClelland, Coordinator of Special Projects; and Janet A. Flint, Curator of Prints and Drawings, for their kindness and cooperation in organizing and assembling this exhibition and catalog. We also wish to recognize the contribution made by Mr. Peter Davidson, of New York City, who was instrumental in establishing contact between the two institutions. It is planned that the exhibition will travel so that others may discover the delicacy and beauty of the graphic works by J. Alden Weir.

W. DOUGLAS STOUT, Chairman
Department of Art
Brigham Young University

J. ALDEN WEIR

An American Printmaker

I have always declined to interpret myself and work and do not know how to go about it. I etched and drew on copper for the sole reason that it had the mystery of a new path. . . .[1]

THE FEW YEARS devoted to etching by Julian Alden Weir, from around 1887 to 1893, fall within the period when he was indeed exploring new paths and new means of expression. Excursions into etching, lithography, engraving, pencil and ink drawings, watercolor, murals and even stained-glass windows, added a new breadth and excitement to his work. And in painting, constant work outdoors in the countryside around his home in Branchville, Connecticut, led him to abandon the dark, smoothly-painted tonalities of his earlier work for the lightened palette and luminosity of a restrained impressionism.[2] It is characteristic of Weir that he approached etching, as he did each new challenge, with a strong sense of integrity and craft.

A young American printmaker's prospects in the last decade of the century were not encouraging as the prevailing taste was for the European paintings and prints which flooded the New York market. Weir is one of a very few American *peintres-graveurs* working at this time, and it was most certainly love of the medium and not hope of gain that engaged his interest.

The actual date of his earliest work in prints is unknown, but he was actively engaged in etching by the summer of 1887. Two impressions, *Dogs on the Hearth No. 1,*[3] dated 1887; and a small portrait of a child (fig. no 10, appendix), undated, but undoubtedly earlier in terms of technical development, bear notations by Weir that they were his first attempts at etching. The command of technique in *Dogs on the Hearth No. 1* would, however, seem to indicate considerable prior experience. Certainly Weir was acquainted with etching techniques through his father, Robert Weir, who was himself an etcher and a collector of old master prints. Weir also collected prints and was particularly fond of etchings by Rembrandt and Van Dyck; one of his earliest essays was a copy of Van Dyck's portrait of Lucas Vorsterman. Friendships with Whistler and Frank Duveneck may have strengthened his interest in etching, but the most direct stimulus probably came from John H. Twachtman. Twachtman, whom Weir met in 1876 while studying at the École des Beaux Arts in Paris, was to become a particularly close friend and working companion. Their mutual interest in etching may have begun in 1881 when Twachtman and his bride were accompanied by Weir and his brother John during a summer sketching tour of Holland. There it was not uncommon for Twachtman to carry several small copper plates and an etching needle with him on their walks. Later, in 1888, after Weir's return to America and his marriage to Anna Baker, the Weir and Twachtman families settled near each other at Branchville where the two artists continued their practice of rambling walks, Weir now joining Twachtman in drawing directly from the landscape on copper plates.[4] It was also in 1888 that Weir acquired a printing press for his country home, sharing there experiments in printing with Twachtman. A summer of etching on the Isle of Man in 1889 produced one of his most charming and fully realized series of etchings (cat. nos. 51-65), a group of eighteen landscapes, and scenes of the harbor and the fishermen. By the winter of 1890 Weir was busy pulling impressions of this series on another press in his new studio in New York. The years 1890 and 1891 were particularly productive, but Weir's world fell apart early in 1892 with the death of his adored wife, Anna.

Only a few prints were made after this: *The Eternal Rest* (cat. nos. 17-22) after a study dated ca. 1892, which must certainly be a portrait of his wife done shortly after her death; and his sole endeavor in engraving, *Arcturus* (cat. no. 31), executed after his return to New York from Chicago where he had worked on mural decorations for the Columbian Exposition of 1892. Some years later, Weir spoke in an interview of his reasons for leaving etching.

For a period of about eight years I was deeply interested in etching and especially drypoint as it was so easy to carry about in one's pocket a half-dozen plates which would fill up odd moments. —I gradually got so interested in a certain charm that etching only possesses, [I] had my own press and would often pull prints to the early hours of the morning. A number of my best plates were ruined by the dropping of a shelf which contained some twenty odd pounds of copper plates, breaking a large bottle of nitric acid Dutch mordant which my foolish man had stood under this shelf. My ardor was somewhat cooled only later to go on again. "The Lamp," an etching and drypoint of a figure reading by night, injured my eyes. At that time I worked at night as painting took a new interest and I gradually dropped etching, hoping and desiring ever since to take it up again.[5]

During this relatively short span of time, Weir produced a remarkable number of prints, over 140, which range from very full, finished studies to incomplete sketches and exercises. Because he seldom printed full editions of his works and because of the accident to a great many of his plates, a considerable number of his etchings and drypoints exist in only a few impressions.[6] Fortunately, comprehensive surveys of his work are to be found in the New York Public Library, the Library of Congress, the Metropolitan Museum of Art, Brigham Young University and, through Brigham Young University's generosity, the National Collection of Fine Arts.

The collections preserve the record of a man who approached printmaking as he approached painting in his later years—as a sensitive and dedicated seeker for a new way of seeing. Essentially self-taught as an etcher, he was not always successful with the medium, faltering occasionally over technical difficulties. But the record of successive states, of changes and experimentations in wiping and printing plates testify to his determination to master all the possibilities inherent in a medium. Weir's interest in technique is shown as well in his willingness to tackle a new medium like lithography when Montagu Marks attempted to establish an American Society of Painter Lithographers in 1896 and urged several artists, Weir among them, to learn the technique. Weir's three lithographs from this period (cat. no. 1) indicate his considerable potential for the medium and one wishes he had continued to work with it.

In etching, Weir could turn easily from a spontaneous, free sketch of a landscape which captured all the essentials in a few strokes, to a highly finished study in tonalities such as *Christmas Greens* (cat. no 2). Drypoint obviously came more easily to him; he drew the drypoint needle through copper with an assurance which does not always appear in his etchings and his interest in luminous shadows and color suggestion was admirably suited to the medium.

But it is Weir's expression rather than technical facility which is so engaging. It is the very lack of highly polished technique and the absence of the bravura of the reproductive etcher of his period, which make them important American works for their time. In an age when facility and an easy sentimentality were too often prized above originality, Weir's prints were remarkable for their honesty, vigor and freshness of vision. While there are echoes of the work of Twachtman and major printmakers of Europe such as Whistler, Besnard and the Barbizon etchers, his prints nevertheless remain essentially and unmistakably his own, personal expression.

Simple scenes—the objects, places and people he loved most in his life—are the subjects of his prints. From accounts of his life, we know that Weir was a gentle, modest man of integrity whose life was happily centered on a quiet family life, close friends, and the countryside in which to paint, walk, or hunt and fish. Most of his studies are drawn from this life—portraits of his family and friends, women engaged in the simple pleasures of sewing and reading, the Connecticut landscape or scenes from his studio in New York. They reflect beautifully Weir's deep reverence and love for the beauties of everyday life.

Weir was not a rebel in art. But, restrained as he was by his own sense of balance and taste and by his respect for European artistic traditions, he did believe firmly in the emergence of a significant school of American painters, liberated from the conventions of the academies. The Society of American Artists and, later, "The Ten"[7] both benefited by his support in their break with academic conservatism, and the example of his own etchings and drypoints undoubtedly fostered a more fertile milieu for the American *peintre-graveur* in this country. During his lifetime, his prints were widely exhibited, praised and awarded prizes; they have since, with a few exceptions, attracted little attention, although as a painter Weir has been recognized as a major figure in the American Impressionist movement. With the coming-of-age of American printmaking and the resultant search into our printmaking past, it is hoped that these fine prints will receive the attention they deserve.

Notes

1. From an essay by Walter Pach, "Peintres-Graveurs Contemporains: M. J. Alden Weir," *Gazette des Beaux-Arts,* vol. 4 (1911), pp. 214-215, translated in *The Life and Letters of J. Alden Weir* by Dorothy Weir Young, Yale University Press, New Haven, 1960, p. 180.

2. Weir's earliest studies were with his father, Robert Weir (1803-1889), a distinguished painter in his own right and for many years Professor of Drawing at the West Point Military Academy. Like his brother John (1841-1926), also a painter and a Professor at Yale's School of Fine Arts, Weir's studies took him to Europe for work with Gérôme at the École des Beaux-Arts in Paris. His early training and his own tastes led him at first to paint mainly studio portraits in an approved manner of the period—precise, careful drawing and modeling, with smoothly-painted surfaces and dark tonalities. The major shift in his work of the nineties to light-filled, vigorously painted landscapes cost him much of his hard-won following. For a full discussion of Weir's life and career see Dorothy Weir Young, *The Life and Letters of J. Alden Weir.*

3. In the collection of Weir's daughter, Caroline Weir Ely.

4. For a discussion of Weir and Twachtman see: Baskett, Mary Welsh, *Prints.* "A Retrospective Exhibition: John Henry Twachtman." Cincinnati: Cincinnati Art Museum, 1966, pp. 32-34.

5. Pach, Walter, *op. cit.*

6. Caroline Weir Ely, schooled in etching by her father, and a highly gifted printer, has fortunately printed a number of Weir plates, usually in editions of twenty-five and signed with her initials, C. W. E., below her father's name.

7. "The Ten" or "Ten American Artists" was a group of artists—which included in addition to Weir—Childe Hassam, Edmund Tarbell, Joseph DeCamp, Willard Metcalf, Thomas Dewing, Frank Benson, Edward Simmons, Robert Reid and John Twachtman. They resigned from their memberships in the Society of American Artists, which they felt had lost its original impetus as a counter-balance to the National Academy, and from 1898 to 1918 exhibited together in nonjuried shows.

CATALOG OF THE EXHIBITION

All prints included in the exhibition are from the collection of Brigham Young University, Provo, Utah. Dimensions are in inches, height preceding width, and, unless otherwise indicated, are those of the plate. Unless indicated by an asterisk (*) following dimensions, prints are reproduced as close to actual size as possible. Signatures referred to are those inscribed in the plate.

Zimmermann numbers refer to *An Essay Towards a Catalogue Raisonné of the Etchings, Dry-points, and Lithographs of Julian Alden Weir* by Agnes Zimmermann; Nelson numbers refer to *The Etchings of J. Alden Weir,* a complete listing of Weir's known prints prepared by Jon Nelson for an exhibition catalog, University of Nebraska Art Galleries, 1967.

Unrecorded states of known prints have been noted under catalog entries and in most cases have been reproduced although not all are included in the exhibition.

1. *Profile Portrait of a Woman Sewing*

Lithograph
12¼ x 9*
Signed lower right: J.A.W.
Zimmermann 2 only state
Nelson 2 only state

2

3

4

2. *Christmas Greens*

Etching and drypoint
$7\frac{7}{8}$ x $5\frac{15}{16}$
Unsigned in plate
Zimmermann 4 iv/v
Nelson 4 iv/v
Proof before the plate was steel-faced

3. *Woman Seated Sewing* 1889

Etching and drypoint
$5\frac{1}{4}$ x $3\frac{3}{4}$
Unsigned in plate
Zimmermann 9 only state
Nelson 9 only state

4. *Woman Embroidering* 1889

Etching
$4\frac{5}{8}$ x $3\frac{1}{8}$
Signed lower right: J.A.W.
Zimmermann 10 only state
Nelson 10 only state

5

6

5. *By Candlelight*

Drypoint
$9\frac{7}{16}$ x $6\frac{1}{4}$
Signed lower left: J A W
Zimmermann 13 only state
Nelson 13 only state
Proof before the plate was steel-fac

6. *The Evening Lamp*

Drypoint and etching
$6\frac{1}{4}$ x $4\frac{5}{8}$ (trimmed to platemark)
Signed lower left: J.A.W.
Zimmermann 14 iv/v
Nelson 14 iv/v

7. *Woman in Black*

Drypoint
7 x 5
Unsigned in plate
Zimmermann 18 i/ii
Nelson 18 i/ii

8. *Portrait of Miss Hoe*

Drypoint
10 x 6⅛ (etched surface)*
Unsigned in plate
Zimmermann 19
Nelson 19

This impression corresponds to Zimmermann's description of the first state, but is before the addition of a drypoint line around the image. Here the line is indicated in pencil and the impression has been trimmed just to this line.

9. *Reflections No. 1*

Drypoint
6⅞ x 5
Signed upper right corner: J.A.W.
Zimmermann 27 only state
Nelson 27 only state

10. *The Lesson*

Etching
$6^{15}/_{16}$ x $4^{7}/_{8}$
Signed lower right: J.A.W.
Zimmermann 46 ii/ii
Nelson 46 ii/ii

11. *The Welsh Doll*

Etching
7⅞ x 6
Unsigned in plate
Zimmermann 47 only state
Nelson 47 only state

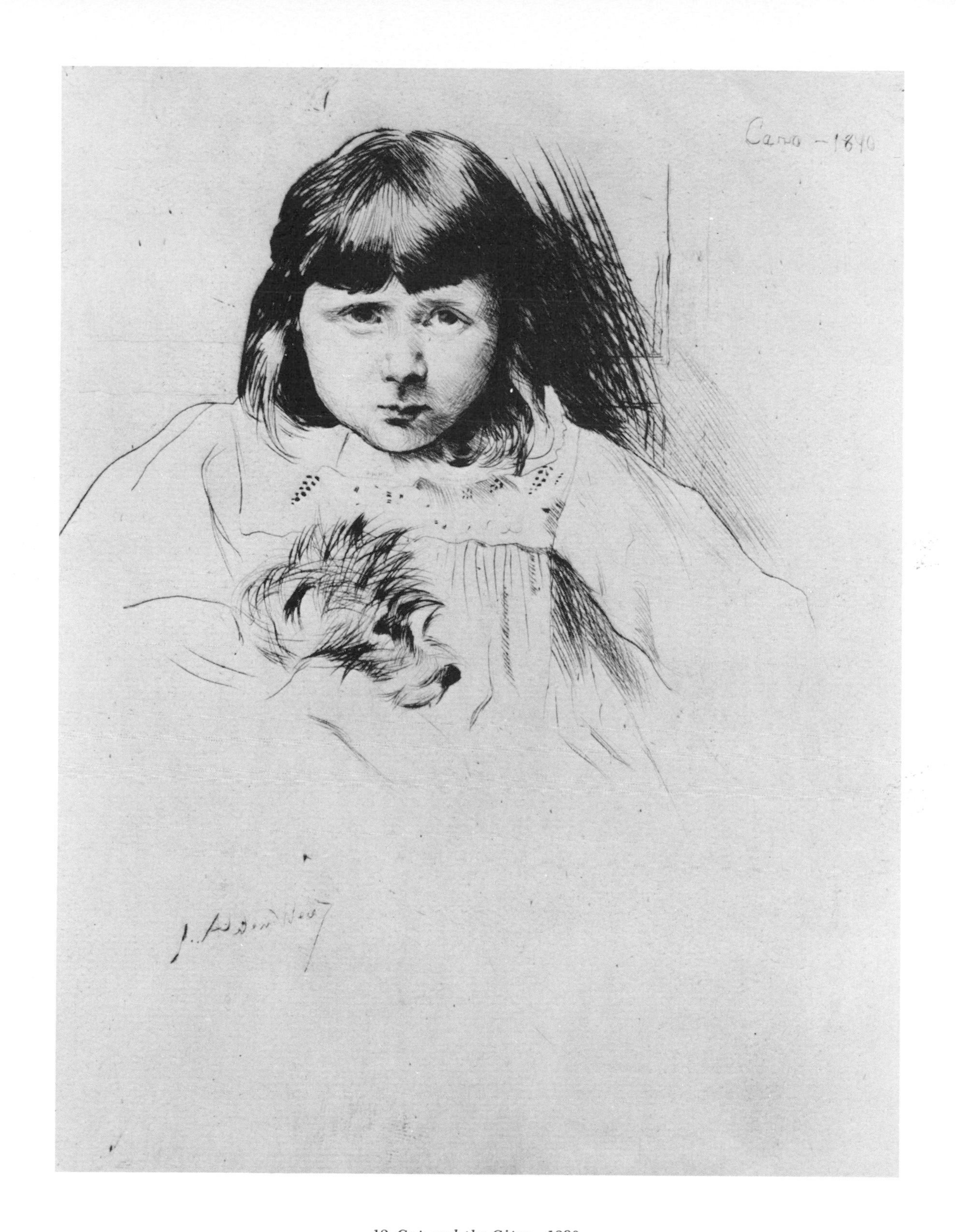

12. *Gyp and the Gipsy* 1890

Drypoint

$7\frac{13}{16}$ x $5\frac{7}{8}$

Signed lower left: J. Alden Weir

Zimmermann 48 only state

Nelson 48 only state

13. *The Little Student* 1890

Drypoint
$4\frac{1}{16}$ x $3\frac{3}{8}$
Signed toward the left, across the window: J. Alden Weir/1890
Zimmermann 54 iii/iv
Nelson 54 iii/iv

14. *The Little Artist* 1890

Etching and drypoint
$6\frac{15}{16}$ x $4\frac{15}{16}$
Signed lower right: J.A.W.
Zimmermann 55 i/ii
Nelson 55 i/ii

15. *The Picture Book*

Etching and drypoint
6⅞ x 5
Signed lower left: J.A.W. (in reverse)
Zimmermann 56 ii/ii
Nelson 56 ii/ii

16. *On the Porch* 1889

Drypoint
$4\frac{7}{8}$ x $4\frac{1}{8}$
Unsigned in plate
Zimmermann 57
Nelson 57

One of three impressions in the Brigham Young Collection undescribed by Zimmermann and Nelson, before the plate was cut down and the edges beveled, reducing the image by $\frac{3}{16}$ on the left and right edges of the plate and $\frac{1}{8}$ at the bottom and top edges. Before beveling, the plate and engraved surface measure $4\frac{7}{8}$ x $4\frac{1}{8}$. After beveling, the plate measures $4\frac{13}{16}$ x $4\frac{1}{16}$ and the engraved surface, $4\frac{9}{16}$ x $3\frac{11}{16}$. This final state was published in the *Gazette des Beaux-Arts,* vol. 4 (1911), between pages 214 and 215.

17. *The Eternal Rest* (First State) ca. 1892

Etching and drypoint
7⅞ x 6$\frac{1}{16}$
Signed lower left: J A W (in monogram enclosed in a circle)
Inscribed in plate lower right: "The eternal rest/to which we shall return/when time has ceased to be/is a pure love"

The major forms are present as they will appear in the final state. The monogram signature appears in the lower left corner and the inscription is lightly etched in the lower right, but without flowers and without the line underneath as in the final state.

18. *The Eternal Rest* (Second State)

Same, but inscription, presumably covered or filled in with a ground, does not appear. The shadow behind the figure and chair has been deepened with additional work.

19. *The Eternal Rest* (Third State)

Same, with additional work on the upper sleeve of the figure and with additional lines on the top of the chair back, behind figure.

Nelson's first state apparently falls between this state and the next. In Nelson's first state, the area under the top arm of the chair has been defined and strengthened with drypoint, forming a strong horizontal V shape.

20. *The Eternal Rest* (Fifth State)

The horizontal V shape, formed between the figure's arm and the top arm of the chair, has now been strongly defined by additional drypoint work. The line defining the lower contour of the arm has been extended to the elbow.

21. *The Eternal Rest* (Sixth State)

The inscription reappears and has been strengthened. A single flower has been added in drypoint to the right of the inscription. This particular impression has a flower drawn in pencil just below the inscription and two flowers in pencil in the lower margin.

22. *The Eternal Rest* (Seventh State)

Nelson 58 ii/ii
Additional flowers have now been added in drypoint to the right and below the inscription. A drypoint line underscores the final line of the inscription. The entire figure has been strengthened with drypoint.

20

"The eternal rest
to which we shall return
when time has ceased to be
is a pure love"

22

"The eternal rest
to which we shall return
when time has ceased to be
is a pure love"

23. *Portrait of Dr. Robert F. Weir* 1891

Drypoint
12 7/16 x 9 1/2*
Unsigned in plate
Zimmermann 58
Nelson 61

This impression represents an uncataloged state between Zimmermann's and Nelson's first and second states. The plate measures 12 7/16 x 9 1/2, as in the first state, but the figure is more fully modeled. Bookshelves and books have been added at the left of the figure, but there are as yet no parallel lines under the left arm and the horizontal lines on the book spines differ from those in Zimmermann's second state. It is before cross-hatching on the tie and before additional work on the cuff of the left sleeve.

Pencil additions indicate some future changes to be made in the plate; the left shoulder line is raised and in subsequent states, the line comes to meet the left collar above the point. Also in pencil is the inscription—Robt F. Weir/Surgeon/S—in the upper left corner.

Robt. F. Weir.
Surgeon.
1891.

24. *Portrait of Dr. Robert F. Weir* 1891

Drypoint
9¼ x 6⁵⁄₁₆
Unsigned in plate
Zimmermann 58
Nelson 61

Apparently an impression of a state after the final Zimmermann state of vi. As described, but the monogram has been removed, as have the fine lines in the lower part of the plate.

25. *Portrait of John F. Weir* 1890

Drypoint
7¾ x 5⅞
Signed lower right: J A W
Zimmermann 60 v/v
Nelson 63 vi/vi

26. *Portrait of Robert Weir* 1891

Drypoint
8 x 6
Unsigned in plate
Zimmermann 61 i/ii
Nelson 64 i/ii

27. *Portrait of Robert Hoe* 1891

Drypoint
10⅞ x 7¹³⁄₁₆*
Signed upper right: J A W (in monogram enclosed in a square)
Zimmerman 63 iv/iv
Nelson 66 iv/iv

[38]

29

28. *Portrait of Mr. Delano*

Etching
8$\frac{15}{16}$ x 7$\frac{1}{16}$
Unsigned in plate
Zimmermann 64 only state
Nelson 67 only state

29. *Portrait of John H. Twachtman* 1888

Etching
6$\frac{5}{8}$ x 5$\frac{1}{16}$
Inscribed in plate lower left: To my friend J.H.T./J.A.W. 1888
This impression bears in addition to the inscription noted by Zimmermann and Nelson, the date "Jan 30th" in the lower right.
Zimmermann 65
Nelson 68

30

30. *Portrait of Theodore Robinson*

Drypoint
6⅞ x 5
Unsigned in plate
Zimmermann 67 only state
Nelson 71 only state

31. *Arcturus* 1892

Engraving
8⅞ x 7⅜
Unsigned in plate
Zimmermann 72 iv/iv
Nelson 76 v/v

32. *The Statue of Liberty*

Etching
$5\frac{7}{16}$ x $3\frac{15}{16}$
Signed lower left: J.A.W.
Zimmermann 73 only state
Nelson 77 only state

33. *Washington Arch No. 1*

Etching
4⅞ x 4
Signed lower left: J A W
Zimmermann 74 only state
Nelson 78 only state

34. *Washington Arch No. 2*

Etching and drypoint
7 x 4 13/16
Unsigned in plate
Zimmermann 75 ii/ii
Nelson 79 ii/ii

35. *My Back Yard No. 1* 1890

Etching and drypoint

$7^{15}/_{16}$ x $5^{15}/_{16}$

Signed lower right: J.A.W.

Zimmermann 76 only state

Nelson 80 only state

36. *My Back Yard No. 2* 1890

Etching
7⅞ x 5$^{15}/_{16}$
Signed lower right: J.A.W.
Zimmermann 77 only state
Nelson 81 only state

37. *The Carpenter's Shop* 1891

Etching

$7\frac{7}{8} \times 5\frac{15}{16}$

Signed on a clapboard at left of lowest step: J.A.W.

Zimmermann 80 only state

Nelson 84 only state

38. *Kitchen Well*

Drypoint
7⁷⁄₁₆ x 5
Signed in tablet with rounded,
pierced top at base of tree:
JAW (in monogram)
Zimmermann 81 only state
Nelson 85 only state

39. *Coon Alley*

Drypoint
5¼ x 3⅞
Signed lower right: J.A.W.
Zimmermann 82 ii/vi
Nelson 86 ii/vi

According to Zimmermann, the signature J.A.W., in lower right, has been erased in the second state. However, it has merely been covered by additional work in the lower right corner and continues to appear in later states.

40. *The Wooden Bridge*

Etching
5 x 6⅞
Unsigned in plate
Zimmermann 84 i/ii
Nelson 88 i/ii

41. *The Stone Bridge*

Etching
4 x $5\frac{15}{16}$
Signed lower right: J.A.W.
Zimmermann 85 only state
Nelson 89 only state

12. *Neighboring Farm*

Etching
10⅞ x 7¾*
Unsigned in plate
Zimmermann 87 only state
Nelson 91 only state

Another proof exists in the Brigham Young Collection, signed by Weir, which carries a pencil inscription, verso, in Weir's handwriting, "farm yard."

13. *The Webb Farm*

Etching and drypoint
5⅝ x 7¾
Signed on stone at foot of ladder: J.A.W.
Zimmermann 88 ii/ii
Nelson 92 ii/ii

Proof impression before the area outlined by drypoint was steel-faced. Impressions exist in the Brigham Young Collection after steel-facing and also in which only the steel-faced portion has been inked, with the plate measurements remaining the same; others in which the print has been trimmed to the drypoint line.

44a

44. *The Barn Lot* 1887

Etching and drypoint

$9\frac{3}{8}$ x $10\frac{3}{4}$*

Signed lower right: J A W/1887 (in reverse) and J. Alden Weir

Zimmermann 90

Nelson 94

There are two impressions in the Brigham Young Collection between Zimmermann's first and second states. In the first of these (no. 44a) the major changes indicated in Zimmermann's first state have been made, but the plate is signed J A W in reverse and below this, 1887 in reverse.

The second impression (no. 44) has considerable additional cross-hatching throughout the field behind and to the right of the stone wall, on the path, and in the bushes on the horizon. Signed as described.

45. *Landscape (Sketch of Fields)*

Etching and roulette work
6 11/16 x 10 3/8*
Unsigned in plate
Nelson 100 only state

In this impression, only the landscape portion has been inked and printed.

46. *The Haystacks*

Etching and drypoint
4 13/16 (right side), 5 1/8 (left side) x 4 1/2 (top and bottom)
Signed lower left: J.A.W.
Zimmermann 93 only state
Nelson 97 only state

Notations on a folder in the Collection of Brigham Young University indicate that at least two impressions were printed from a plate with a straight base. Their whereabouts are unknown.

47. *Dogs on the Hearth No. 2*

Etching
16¾ x 20$^{11}/_{16}$*
Unsigned in plate
Zimmermann 97 only state
Nelson 102 only state

48. *Dutch Schnapps*

Drypoint
5¼ x 3⅞
Signed on rim of goblet: J A W
Zimmermann 99 only state
Nelson 104 only state

49

50

51

19. *Bas Meudon No. 2* 1889
Etching
$3\frac{7}{8}$ x $5\frac{5}{16}$
Signed lower right: J.A.W.
Zimmermann 101 only state
Nelson 106 only state

50. *Liverpool Docks* 1889
Etching
$3\frac{15}{16}$ x $5\frac{15}{16}$
Unsigned in plate
Zimmermann 103 only state
Nelson 108 only state

51. *Title Page—Isle of Man Series* 1889
Etching and drypoint
$3\frac{7}{16}$ x $5\frac{3}{8}$ (etched surface)
Unsigned in plate
Zimmermann 106 only state
Nelson 111 only state

52. *Harbor—Isle of Man* 1889

Etching
4 x 5$\frac{15}{16}$
Unsigned in plate
Zimmermann 107 only state
Nelson 112 only state

53. *Boats at Peel—Isle of Man* 1889

Etching
11$\frac{7}{8}$ x 8$\frac{15}{16}$ (trimmed within platemark)*
Unsigned in plate
Zimmermann 108 i/ii
Nelson 113 i/ii

54. *Boats at Low Tide—Isle of Man* 1889

Etching

$6^{15}/_{16}$ x $4^{15}/_{16}$

Signed lower left: J.A.W.

Inscribed in plate lower right: Peel (in reverse) /June 18, 1889 rather than "J.A.W." in reverse as noted by Zimmermann and Nelson.

Zimmermann 109 only state

Nelson 114 only state

55. *Boats at Port Erin—Isle of Man* 1889

Etching

4 x $5^{15}/_{16}$

Unsigned in plate

Zimmermann 110 only state

Nelson 115 only state

56. *Port Erin—Isle of Man* 1889

Etching

4 x 6

Unsigned in plate

Zimmermann 111 only state

Nelson 116 only state

55

56

57. *Castle Rushen—Isle of Man* 1889

Etching
8¾ x 11⅞*
Signed lower center: J. Alden Weir (in reverse)
Zimmermann 113 ii/ii
Nelson 118 ii/ii

58. *Street in Peel—Isle of Man* 1889

Etching
$6\frac{7}{16}$ x $4\frac{1}{2}$ (etched surface)
Signed lower left: J A W/1889
Zimmermann 115 only state
Nelson 120 only state

59. *Fisherman's Hut—Isle of Man* 1889

Etching
8⅞ x 11$^{3}/_{16}$*
Unsigned in plate
Zimmermann 116 only state
Nelson 121 only state

60. *Fisherman's Hut on the Hill—Isle of Man* 1889

Etching
5 x 7
Unsigned in plate
Zimmermann 117 only state
Nelson 122 only state

61

61. *Fisherman's Hut, Interior—Isle of Man* 1889

Etching

4 15/16 x 6 15/16

Unsigned in plate

Zimmermann 118 only state

Nelson 123 only state

62. *Manx Cats—Isle of Man* 1889

Etching

4 x 6

Unsigned in plate

Zimmermann 120 only state

Nelson 125 only state

63. *Glebe Farm—Isle of Man* 1889

Etching

3¾ x 5¾

Unsigned in plate

Zimmermann 121 only state

Nelson 126 only state

62

63

64. *Farm-Yard—Isle of Man* 1889

Drypoint
$4\frac{15}{16}$ x $6\frac{15}{16}$
Unsigned in plate
Zimmermann 122 only state
Nelson 127 only state

65. *Sulby Glen—Isle of Man* 1889

Etching
9 x 12*
Unsigned in plate
Zimmermann 123 only state
Nelson 128 only state

Appendix

The Appendix includes a number of previously uncataloged prints which are listed and illustrated. These are mainly unfinished works, of historical interest but not representative of Weir's best work, and therefore have not been included in the exhibition.

Figure 1

Figure 1. *Around the Table*

Etching

3⅜ x 4⅞

Unsigned in plate

Inscribed in pencil verso: Around the Table

Figure 2

Figure 3

Figure 2. *Artist Seated at Easel*
Etching
4 13/16 x 3 3/8 (trimmed)
Unsigned in plate

Figure 3. *Convalescing*
Etching
2 5/16 x 3 1/4 (trimmed)
Unsigned in plate
Inscribed lower right corner of mat:
Convalescing

Figure 4. *Dreaming No. 2*

Etching
8½ x 7 (trimmed)
Signed in pencil lower right: J. Alden Weir
Inscribed in pencil verso: Destroyed

Figure 5. *Eventide*

Etching
11⅞ x 8⅞*
Unsigned in plate
Inscribed in pencil lower right margin: Eventide

Figure 6. *Fashionable Cape*

Etching
7 x 5
Unsigned in plate
Inscribed in pencil lower right margin: Fashionable Cape

Figure 7. *Portrait of a Man*

Drypoint
6⅞ x 5
Unsigned in plate

Figure 8. *Reading By the Window*
Etching
6 15/16 x 5
Unsigned in plate
Inscribed in pencil lower right margin: Reading By the Window

Figure 9. *Reading Out of Doors*

Etching and drypoint
6⅝ x 9*
Unsigned in plate
Inscribed in pencil lower right margin: Reading Out of Doors

Figure 10. *Seated Child*

Etching
5 x 4 3/16
Signed on sole of child's shoe: J A Weir
Inscribed in ink lower right margin: first attempt at etching/J.A.W.

Figure 11. *Seated Model*

Etching
$5^{13}/_{16}$ x $4^{1}/_{4}$ (trimmed)
Unsigned in plate

Figure 12. *Sewing on the Porch*

Drypoint
$4\frac{15}{16}$ x $3\frac{3}{16}$
Unsigned in plate
Inscribed in pencil lower right margin: Sewing on the Porch

Figure 13. *Sketch By the Window No. 2*

Etching
$6\frac{3}{4}$ x $5\frac{1}{8}$ (trimmed)
Signed lower right: J A W
Signed in pen lower left margin: J. Alden Weir
Inscribed in pencil lower right corner of mat: Sketch
By the Window No. 2

Figure 14. *Sketches—Two Heads*

Etching
6⅜ x 8$\frac{5}{16}$*
Unsigned in plate
Inscribed in pencil lower right margin: Sketches—2 Heads

Figure 15. *Woman and Child, Seated*

Drypoint

$6\frac{13}{16}$ x $4\frac{15}{16}$

Signed lower left: J. Alden Weir

Figure 16. *Woman in Big Hat*

Drypoint
7 x 5
Unsigned in plate
Inscribed in pencil lower right margin: Woman in Big Hat

Figure 17. *Woman Out of Doors*

Etching

6⅞ x 5

Inscribed in pencil lower right margin: Woman Out of Doors

Figure 18

Figure 19

Figure 18. *Woman Resting*
Etching
8¾ x 6⅞
Unsigned in plate
Inscribed in pencil lower right margin: Woman Resting

Figure 19. *Woman With a Muff*
Drypoint
7⅞ x 5⅞
Unsigned in plate
Inscribed in pencil lower right margin: Woman With a Muff

Figure 20

Figure 21

Selected Bibliography

Archives of American Art, Letters, clippings, list of prints compiled by Dorothy Weir Young, and other material on microfilm.

Baskett, Mary Welsh, *Prints.* "A Retrospective Exhibition: John Henry Twachtman." Cincinnati: Cincinnati Art Museum, 1966.

Baur, John I. H., *Leaders of American Impressionism: Mary Cassatt, Childe Hassam, John H. Twachtman, J. Alden Weir.* Brooklyn: Brooklyn Museum, 1937.

Baur, John I. H., *Revolution and Tradition in Modern American Art.* Cambridge, Mass.: Harvard University Press, 1951.

Cary, Elizabeth Luther, "Etched Work of J. Alden Weir," *Scribners,* vol. 68 (1920), pp. 507-512.

Ely, Caroline Weir, *Catalogue of an Exhibition of Etchings by J. Alden Weir.* New York: Frederick Keppel and Co., 1927.

Memorial Exhibition of the Works of Julian Alden Weir. New York: Metropolitan Museum of Art, 1924.

Millet, J. B., ed., *Julian Alden Weir: An Appreciation of His Life and Works.* New York: The Century Club, 1921. (Reprinted without substantive change as The Phillips Publications, No. 1, New York, 1922)

Nelson, Jon, *The Etchings of J. Alden Weir.* Lincoln, Nebraska: University of Nebraska, 1967.

New York Times, December 9, 1919, p. 17 (obituary); December 10, 1919, p. 12 (editorial); April 18, 1920, VI, 8; March 17, 1924, p. 51; March 23, 1924, IV, 10; March 27, 1927, VII, 11; January 6, 1929, VIII, 13; March 24, 1935, VIII, 7; October 18, 1942, VIII, 9 (reviews of exhibitions).

Pach, Walter, "Peintres-Graveurs Contemporains: M. J. Alden Weir," *Gazette des Beaux-Arts,* vol. 4 (1911), pp. 214-215.

Weitenkampf, Frank, *American Graphic Art.* New ed. rev. and enl. New York: The Macmillan Company, 1924.

Weitenkampf, Frank, "Weir's Excursions into Print-Land," *Arts and Decoration,* vol. 12 (1920), pp. 208-209.

Young, Dorothy Weir, *The Life and Letters of J. Alden Weir.* New Haven: Yale University Press, 1960.

Young, Mahonri M., *An Appreciation.* "J. Alden Weir 1852-1919: Centennial Exhibition." New York: American Academy of Arts and Letters, 1952.

Zimmermann, Agnes, *An Essay Towards a Catalogue Raisonné of the Etchings, Dry-Points, and Lithographs of Julian Alden Weir.* "The Metropolitan Museum of Art Papers." vol. 1, part 2, 1923.

Zimmermann, Agnes, "Julian Alden Weir, His Etchings," *Print Collectors Quarterly,* vol. 10 (1923), pp. 288-308.

Figure 20. *Farm On a Hill*
Etching
4 x 6
Unsigned in plate
Inscribed in pencil lower right margin: Farm On a Hill

Figure 21. *Landscape*
Drypoint
5 x 7⅜
Unsigned in plate

Index of Titles

Reference is to catalog number; figure numbers refer to appendix.